Ja Morant: The Inspiring Story of One of Basketball's All-Star Point Guards

An Unauthorized Biography

By: Clayton Geoffreys

Table of Contents

Foreword

Since being selected with the second overall pick of the 2019 NBA Draft, Ja Morant has consistently impressed fans across the league. So much so, that he won the 2020 Rookie of the Year Award. In his rookie season, Ja finished averaging 17.8 points per game, along with 7.3 assists per game. Every year since entering the league, Ja has become a better and better player. In 2022, he was selected for his very first All-Star nomination. It is unlikely that it'll be his last. Thank you for purchasing *Ja Morant: The Inspiring Story of One of Basketball's All-Star Point Guards*. In this unauthorized biography, we will learn Ja Morant's incredible life story and impact on the game of basketball. Hope you enjoy and if you do, please do not forget to leave a review!

Also, check out my website at claytongeoffreys.com to join my exclusive list where I let you know about my latest books. To thank you for your purchase, you can go to my site to download a free copy of *33 Life Lessons: Success Principles, Career Advice & Habits of Successful People*. In the book, you'll learn from some of the greatest thought leaders of different industries on what it takes to become successful and how to live a great life.

Cheers,

Clayton Geoffreys

Visit me at www.claytongeoffreys.com

Introduction

The NBA, throughout its entire history, has seen its fair share of different players with a good combination of positional size, athleticism, and talent. In that regard, the greatest stars in the history of the league have always been all about the potential that these players possessed before they even made it to the NBA. And most of these players were drafted as future franchise stars precisely because they had the potential to be great.

Some of the greatest players that were drafted based on their potential include names such as Michael Jordan, LeBron James, Shaquille O'Neal, Derrick Rose, and Anthony Davis, all of whom were players that already had the size, athleticism, and talent for greatness. And even if some players were not yet ready to take the league by storm when they were drafted, names like Kobe Bryant, Giannis Antetokounmpo, and James

Harden had the potential to become great as well but needed time to develop.

In that regard, teams usually define potential as a combination of skills, size, athleticism, and drive. As long as the player has these things covered, he will surely have a chance to become one of the greatest players. And, for most teams, drafting a player with the right combination of skills, size, and athleticism is already more than enough to secure a bright future for the franchise, especially if that player is competitive enough to want to give his all in order to be great.

One such player that comes into mind concerning his potential and his opportunity to be great is the point guard named Ja Morant. His potential for greatness comes from the fact that he has everything required of a franchise player ready to take a team to heights greater than it has ever reached before.

When Ja Morant was drafted by the Memphis Grizzlies back in 2019, he was the second overall pick.

In most cases, a player of his caliber should have been the top overall pick. However, he was in the same draft class with the physical prodigy named Zion Williamson. But that did not stop Ja from becoming arguably the greatest player of his draft class as of this writing.

The Memphis Grizzlies chose Ja Morant not because he was the next best player behind Zion Williamson. Rather, they chose him because they needed a point guard that could carry them to a new chapter after the organization had finally decided to completely move on from the grindhouse era of the Grizzlies when they parted ways with former franchise point guard Mike Conley.

When Morant entered the league, everyone was excited about him because he was already a highlight machine back in college. Despite the fact that the entire nation was more excited about Zion's ability to put on freakish feats of athleticism in college, Ja was just as exciting in his second year with Murray State because he could do it all.

Described as a player molded from the same cloth as Russell Westbrook when it comes to his explosiveness, Ja Morant was always an athlete as prodigious as any other in the NBA. At 6'3" and with a slight frame, he played bigger than he was back in college because he could outjump almost every other player in the nation. Able to simply rise up for spectacular dunks or perform jaw-dropping blocks on players much bigger than he was, it was as if he had pogo sticks for legs.

Thanks to his athleticism and innate talent as a point guard, Ja Morant averaged 24.5 points and ten assists in his final year with Murray State and became the first Division I player to ever average at least 20 points and ten assists for a full season. And because he was also putting up triple-doubles in college, people were looking to him as the second coming of Russel

Westbrook, just as how Trae Young was thought to be the second coming of Steph Curry.

But as Morant continued to strut his stuff in the NBA, he steadily proved that he was someone much more unique than what people thought. It might have been true that Morant possessed the same nuclear athleticism that made Russell Westbrook special in his prime; however, he also had a different kind of feel that made it clear that he was going to be the first player of his kind. Possessing the athleticism of Russell Westbrook, the pace-changing of Derrick Rose, and the decision-making of Chris Paul, Morant was steadily looking like a new breed of point guard in the NBA. On top of that, he also possessed the craftiness and fearlessness of an all-time great scoring guard named Allen Iverson, who, despite his slight frame, was capable of scoring at will, even against bigger opponents.

But while he might have showcased a well-roundedness in his game, orant's main weapon was still his athleticism. Using his athletic gifts, he could dunk on opponents with ease. He also became popular for his almost-poster dunks, which would have been all-time greats had the ball gone in. And while some of his dunk attempts on bigger players did not go through the hoop, his fearlessness as an attacker was evident.

Despite Morant being known for his athleticism, he showed early signs of his mastery of the fundamentals of the sport. He was crafty with the ball in his hands, and being athletic added to his shiftiness while dribbling the ball and navigating his way through defenders. Ja could make it to the basket with ease because of his long strides, quick feet, and crafty handles. This led to him winning the Rookie of the Year award overwhelmingly to the point that he was one first-place vote from winning it unanimously.

However, while most players with his athleticism would almost always attempt a strong finish regardless of the type of defense near the basket, Morant proved himself capable of hitting floaters by stopping on a dime in a paint. In that regard, he had a bit of Derrick Rose in him because of his mastery of the floater.

But while some of the greatest athletes in the NBA took time to develop their jump shot, as they only did so when they realized that they were getting slower with age, Morant was already proving himself as a capable shooter in his third year in the NBA. He was not someone defenders were willing to give enough space outside the perimeter because he was capable of draining three-pointers. This only made him a tougher player to cover, as he became a 25-point threat on a nightly basis.

As impressive as Morant's individual rise was, the more impressive part was the fact that he carried the Grizzlies alongside his improvement. In just his second year in the league, he was able to lead Memphis to the playoffs after defeating the league's best point guard and two-time MVP Stephen Curry in the play-in game for the eighth seed in the West. Then, in his third year in the NBA, he, along with the Memphis Grizzlies was showing everyone in the league that they could be championship contenders as well. Beating powerhouse opponents left and right, the Grizzlies went on a double-digit win streak during the middle portion of the season, as Morant's leadership and ability to destroy opponents through his scoring and playmaking were essential to their success. There was no doubt that he was going to be an All-Star.

For all the jaw-dropping dunks he performed in college and the NBA, Morant was not one of the "chosen ones" coming out of high school. He was barely recruited and was not even ranked by some of the best names, such as *ESPN* or *Rivals*. He watched as his friends were getting recruited by some of the best programs in the country. He was only able to get to

Murray State, a mid-major program because he was discovered by accident.

Despite that, Morant worked his hardest to make sure that he would become someone the entire nation would know. With his athletic feats and refined skills, he took the nation by storm during his sophomore year in college. And that was when he became a household name that needed to work hard to get to the point where he was touted as a future star in the NBA. He became the type of player that everyone in the Grizzlies organization hoped he would become. But the surprising part was that he did it in no time, as he developed at a rapid pace without forgetting about carrying the team on his back during his development. He became a star in only his third season in the NBA, but he could also be a superstar, especially after regarding his potential and drive as a competitor.

The future is bright for Ja Morant and the Memphis Grizzlies. As he is already one of the best young players the NBA has to offer today, at the pace he is improving and barring any injuries, he will become one of the best players in the league in a few years. Of course, the more important part of the equation is his team. As long as he can carry the Grizzlies to greater heights while showcasing his greatness as an individual, there is a good chance that he would become one of the all-time greats. After all, that is what a franchise player is supposed to do.

Chapter 1: Childhood and Early Life

Temetrius Jamel "Ja" Morant was born on August 10, 1999, in Dalzell, South Carolina. While it took a long time for Ja to take off as a basketball player, he could thank his parents' basketball genes for his natural skills and athletic gifts that were perfect for the sport. That is because his parents, Tee and Jamie Morant, were both talented basketball players in their own right. Jamie, back when she was in her younger years, played point guard in high school. In college, she was good enough to make the softball team.[i] Being an athlete allowed her to meet Ja's father, Tee, who himself was supposed to pursue a career in basketball as well because he was arguably the more talented athlete of the two parents.

Tee Morant played basketball at Hillcrest High School, a member of the team that won the state championship during the 1992-93 season, led by Ray Allen, one of the greatest shooting guards of all time. While Tee could not get offers from some of the best programs in the nation, he was still good enough to make it to NAIA Claflin College in Orangeburg, where he became a constant double-double threat. Tee was unable to get to the NBA after playing basketball in a smaller collegiate program, but he was still good enough to play semi-professionally.

At first, he tried to pursue a career of playing professionally overseas; however, when he found out that Jamie was pregnant with Ja, he decided to forego his dreams as a professional basketball player and opted to stay home with his family instead. Tee pursued a career in a small town as a barber while taking an active role in raising and training his son in basketball.[ii]

Ja was as young as three years old when he started becoming obsessed with the game of basketball, the best part being that he always had his father with him to train him, as not all young players get a chance to learn from a former college basketball player good enough to receive offers from overseas.

Throughout his younger years, Ja and his father trained relentlessly in the small quarter-court in the family's backyard. But Ja was relentless as a child; all while his father had him undergo advanced drills that children were not supposed to go through. He dribbled through caution cones, improved his footwork using ladder drills, and learned how to move laterally using resistance bands. And Ja loved every minute of it because he was so obsessed with basketball. "If there was a ball bouncing," said Tee, "he wanted to be around it."[iv]

Of course, Morant could also thank his DNA because he did have the genes of capable athletes running through his veins. Coupled with the training that his father gave him, it was easy for him to learn how to play basketball at a young age while also honing the fundamental skills and physical movements needed in the sport. And Tee was especially proud of the genetic lineage that helped create a super athlete like his son.

"The DNA was incredible," Tee said. "I will claim our DNA is incredible. Did I say our DNA is incredible? He's got an incredible genetic line as far as athletics. But once he took the basketball, it was all basketball, all workouts, all everything."[ii]

But it was Jamie who knew beforehand that her son was going to be great because she was already hyping Ja up before he was even born. One could say that this was merely a case of proud parents being proud of their own genetics, but both Tee and Jamie were eventually right about their child.

"My wife will tell you she knew Ja was going to be great when he was in her belly," Tee said. "She actually said that. I guess that's that woman intuition. But, at the same time, you second-guessing her now?"[iii]

Factoring in how Tee was someone who knew how to drill the fundamentals into a child's brain, one could easily see how Ja was able to pick up the game of basketball faster than most other kids. And it even came to a point when other kids around the neighborhood began joining him on drills, considering that he lived in a particularly small town with a small population.

"It's a very small town, the country, a lot of woods. But almost everybody around there know each other. That's why I'm a big family person," Ja said.[i]

Even though Morant's early development as a basketball player revolved around the drills that he underwent with his father and the other kids in the neighborhood, one of the things that he developed early on as well was his confidence: something that led to his performance in the NBA, like he knew he was the best player out on the floor. Its development, however, was not basketball-related. Instead, Tee had

Ja perform in front of crowds whenever possible. This allowed him to learn what it was like to be in front of a lot of people without fearing whether or not his performance was up to par. And he performed in all sorts of crowds, no matter how big or small his audience was.

"Ja was full-blown Michael Jackson with the jacket, the hat, doing all of it," Carol Morant, Ja's aunt, said. "We would call him out, and he would get in full performance and have everybody watch his performances. So, he's been performing for a long time in different capacities. He's known how to entertain from a young age."[i]

While most people would say that Ja performing and dancing in front of people did not matter in his basketball development, the young Morant credits his early experiences when it comes to performing under pressure. Other people tend to fold under pressure no matter how good or talented they may be, but Morant learned early on that he was someone who thrived under the spotlight. "I don't be nervous," Ja said. "So, I feel like that helped. They used to make me dance sometimes, but I got used to it. I already knew what he was going to say and stuff, so I'd just do it on my own."[iii]

Due to his early development as a player, Morant was playing in leagues meant for seven to nine-year-old kids at the age of six. There were no leagues made for children his age, and that was why he was forced to play against kids that were two or three years older. Despite the apparent difference in size, he stood out and was capable of scoring baskets over larger players. And, as Tee remarked, his son was already good enough to make passes unexpected of any six-year-old. Ja was so good at his age that many wondered why he was even playing against kids. The way he was dribbling and shooting the ball was already exceptional for someone as young as he was. And this was something that everyone in the neighborhood witnessed.

At the age of nine, Morant was already dominating the league meant for kids his age. His self-esteem and confidence allowed him to drain shot after shot against bigger defenders. And he was still a comparatively small boy at that time. It did not matter because he could make three-pointers and would even use WWE superstar John Cena's "You can't see me" taunt after draining his shots.[i]

While his father was not particularly fond of his showboating, he was still able to perform at his best and went on to finish 25 or more points on a regular basis. Morant was already a kid capable of putting on a show during his childhood years while playing against kids much older and bigger than he was at that time. This was a nine-year-old boy showboating against ten or 11-year old children. But even though he was performing at his best at his age by scoring plenty of points and making the right passes, he was his harshest critic. The coaches would often tell the players to rate their performance on the court after a game. Even if Morant played well, he was the first to tell anyone that he needed to improve by giving himself a low grade. And this was something he picked up from his father.

"There's a lot of times we'd get out the van I'd be like, 'Why the [expletive] you give yourself a five? You had like three turnovers; you had like 25 points and eight assists,'" Tee said. "But that was just me being real. I never gave him the seal of approval. I always told him he was overrated and all that. My wife would be like, 'Why you always tell him that?' I'd be like, 'Because I got to keep him hungry.' And now, people asking me, 'Why's your boy so hungry?' And I say, 'Because I haven't been feeding him [expletive].'"iii

Ja also learned how to look up to NBA players so that he could find ways to improve. The young Morant started following Russell Westbrook, who was still on the rise at that time. One of the things he picked up from Westbrook was his quick dribble free-throw jumper. This used to be a shot that Russ could make on a regular basis during his prime years in the NBA. Morant knew that this was an unstoppable shot that he could add to his game, and, as his uncle, Roger Morant, said, knowing how to pick habits up from NBA superstars was a good sign that his basketball IQ was improving.

Ja idolized Russ so much at that time, not because Westbrook was an athletic beast. Instead, he saw himself in Westbrook because of the killer mentality that the latter seemed to have. The dog mentality was something that Ja Morant grew up with, especially because he was neither the biggest nor the most talented player in the leagues that he played in as a young boy. And looking up to Westbrook allowed him to hone a similar kind of dog mentality that allowed him to show no fear when attacking other people.[iii]

While he may have looked up to NBA players, the tight-knit community he grew up with in South Carolina allowed Ja to look up to a lot of other people as well. Specifically, he did not only listen to his father but also his mom, who he originally did not know was a good player. Jamie had to drive him all the way to her hometown high school to show her the awards she won back when she was a high school point guard. And, since then, he began looking up to his mother as well.

Moreover, the fact that he grew up in a small community also allowed Morant to focus on basketball. The Morant family built a small backyard basketball court that eventually grew bigger as the demands on it increased. It started out with Ja and Tee training as a duo, but the neighborhood kids began joining them in their drills. It soon reached a point where 50 to 60 people would be in the backyard just enjoying basketball, eating barbecue, and spending time together.[i] In a way, the basketball-centric approach that the community possessed had started out with the Morant household and the young boy that would soon become a star in the NBA.

The fact that he grew up in a small community also allowed Ja to focus on trying to get better. Basketball was his whole life because there were not a lot of things to do in his hometown. He watched college basketball games and even went on to use whatever he learned from NBA and college players on the basketball video games he played as a young boy. And his approach in life allowed him to grow in terms of his basketball IQ while learning more and more about the game and its different nuances.

Despite the fact that he was growing in skill and basketball IQ, Morant was not growing fast enough physically. He had always been a short and scrawny kid ever since he started playing basketball. However, while most of his peers were steadily growing, he was doing so at a slower rate. By the time Ja was in his middle school years, he was only 5'5".

Because Ja was still a bit short compared to his peers when he was in middle school, that was the time that Tee focused a lot of the young man's training on knowing how to shoot step-back jumpers. Learning step-backs allowed him to create enough space and separation to get a shot off without getting it blocked. And it worked well enough during his younger years.

While he may have been quite short during his middle school years, Morant still saw a growth spurt that allowed him to play better than ever. By the time he finished his middle school years, he was already 5'10", a height that was good enough for incoming high school players. Then again, the problem with him at that time was the lack of exposure. This trend continued until his high school years.

Chapter 2: High School Career

When Ja Morant reached high school, he did not have the most productive start in his career. The young boy started out on the junior varsity team at Crestwood High School in Sumter, South Carolina. And while other players would not find it a good thing to start in the JV, Ja and his father thought of it as a blessing because it allowed the young boy to find his bearing and continue to train more without the added pressure of trying to star in the varsity team. As such, a lot of the time Ja spent on the junior varsity team as a freshman was focused on individual backyard training sessions with his father. Of course, as he was already growing into his body, that was the time when Tee noticed that his son was also getting more and more athletic. It was the perfect time for the younger Morant to perform drills that were aimed at improving his vertical leap, which would become arguably the most impressive aspect of his game when he got to the NBA.

Because of how Tee thought that his son needed a more focused style of training, Ja did not spend a lot of time with his AAU team, thought it allowed Morant to connect with one of the most exciting players of his generation. And what the world did not know was that he and this player would get picked as the top two players in the 2019 NBA Draft.

It was during the summer before his sophomore year that Morant joined a grassroots AAU team called the South Carolina Hornets. The Hornets were composed of players that were within the Southern Carolina area, as the team was based out of Columbia. And another kid named Zion Williamson, an incoming freshman from Spartanburg, joined the team as well.

"Zion was always a mild-mannered kid, never showed much expression," Tee said. "He was probably 6-foot-3 then. He had hops, but he didn't have the hops that he possesses now."[iii]

Zion Williamson attributes his popularity, in part, to the viral dunks he put up during his college career at Duke and after putting up dominating numbers in the NBA during the early part of his career. Compared to Morant's level of athleticism, Williamson was an even bigger super athlete that could jump higher than anyone else despite his huge frame.

Because Zion was already such an impressive player at that time, he only spent a year with the South Carolina Hornets before moving on to an even bigger AAU program. Meanwhile, Morant stayed with the Hornets. He was teammates with Williamson for only one summer, but that was a summer that Morant used more for training instead of playing with his AAU team.

Meanwhile, Tee had Ja doing everything possible to improve his son's athleticism. The younger Morant's height was nearing six feet at that time, but there was no assurance that he would become taller than that. That was why it was important for him to improve his athleticism, as doing so would allow him to make up for his slight and shorter frame.

In the family backyard, Ja was doing things such as resistance parachutes and jumping on tractor tires. Hill sprints were also quite common, as the young man only continued to improve athletically. He was becoming faster, all while his vertical leaping ability was improving as well. The training may have seemed a bit too basic, but it helped Morant during his formative years as a basketball player that was still growing into his body.

After spending a summer training with his father and improving his athletic abilities on top of continuing to grow in terms of his skills, Morant considered an offer to play for the varsity team when his high school coach Dwyane Edwards thought that the young man was ready to play on the main squad. But the Morants eventually declined the offer of elevating him to the senior team. Tee said that Ja needed to learn more while playing for the junior varsity team. The younger Morant would have surely earned a lot of playing time with the varsity team, but the fact was that he still wanted to grow on the JV team, considering that he was his strictest and harshest critic. It was important to stay one more season. And staying with the JV team proved to be useful for him.

By the time Morant was at last elevated to the varsity team, he had begun dominating the field. Standing six feet tall, Morant used his combination of athleticism, skill, and IQ to do it all out on the floor. He was scoring, rebounding, defending, and making plays as an all-around point guard that sometimes looked like a fundamentally sound version of Russell Westbrook because he was putting up triple-doubles on a regular basis.

"If you put four other guys around him, he's gonna make them better," Edwards said. "I always tell them all the time, that's why I always liked Magic Johnson, because Magic always got the most out of his guys, and that's Ja. To be honest, you could have an average player, but playing on a team with Ja Morant, he could make it seem like you're a pretty good player because he's going to get them involved."[iii]

Morant was indeed like Magic Johnson while putting up Russell Westbrook numbers during his time with the varsity team. During his final two years in high school, he averaged 27 points, eight rebounds, and eight assists, as he was doing it all for Crestwood. Morant ran the offense like a virtuoso point guard and also made all of his other teammates better with his passing, playmaking, and decision-making.

Of course, Morant was the perfect point guard for his team. They ran a run-and-gun offense that liked to push the tempo. When playing the half-court, they also relied on plenty of ball movement. And the fact that Ja was the one running the offense was what allowed Crestwood to perform at its best.

"I had an offense, but if you've got Ja Morant and you got the floor spacing or on a break or whatever, he's gonna make the best decision when it comes down to trying to get that basket," Edwards said. "He had that freedom with me."[iii]

Even without a coach's trained eye, Morant's impact on the floor was obvious. Casual fans could understand that he was the general leading the troops whenever he was the one running the offense. There were even instances when he was the one calling the timeouts and the plays for his team. He had that kind of freedom under an offense that offered him a lot of leeway. Even though Morant was dominating South Carolina, he was never content with what he was doing. Edwards was always the first to rave about his star player's work ethic because he was frequently requesting to keep the school gym open on Sundays so that he could train by himself. And after games and practices, he and his father often spent time doing individual training sessions in their backyard while assessing where they could improve next.

Surprisingly, Morant was on no one's radar. It was not due to the fact that he was playing in a smaller region in South Carolina, as some of his other peers in the area were actually receiving scholarship offers from Division I schools following their junior years. But it was surprising that Morant was not getting any. The only offers he got after his junior year were from South Carolina State and Maryland Eastern-Shore. It was not as if Morant did not have the numbers and the feats to prove that he belonged in college. He was putting up amazing numbers while still improving athletically at that time. Then again, Morant was quite small for his age, barely six feet tall. And while he had greatly improved athletically, he did not dunk the ball in games at that point in his life because his hops were still developing, and his height made it more difficult for him to reach the hoop regularly.

"We was stumped pretty much," Tee said. "It felt like our hands was tied, and somebody was like beating the hell out of our child. He's putting everything out there. He's showing the work. He's showing how good he is. But at the same time, what are scouts seeing that we're not seeing?"[iii]

Despite the fact that none of the scouts from the bigger programs were seeing something special in Morant, he did not lose hope. He continued to work harder and harder. Jamie did her best to make her son understand that he was beneath no one. Meanwhile, Tee kept on telling his son that his time would come because "cream will always rise to the top."

As fate would have it, Ja Morant was discovered by a coach who was hungry both figurately and literally. James Kane was working as an assistant coach for Murray State at that time, and he was the personality that helped turn Morant's life around when he happened to stumble on the point guard by accident.

In July of 2016, just as Morant was entering his final year in high school, Kane drove a quarter of a day from Kentucky to Spartanburg Day School in South Carolina to attend a combine for high school players. This was the same school that Zion Williamson was attending, as the young boy was already getting offers from different programs all over the nation even though he was only entering his junior year in high school. But Kane was not there for Williamson because there was no way a smaller school like Murray could convince him to sign up with them. Instead, he was there to check out Tevin Brown, a smooth-shooting wing from Alabama.

Hungry to find his place as a coach in college, Kane was willing to do everything it took. Some of the other coaches of the best schools were taking chartered flights, but he had to drive to recruit players to join his program. But it was that fateful drive to Spartanburg that allowed him to have a chance encounter with an overlooked player from a high school in Sumter.

Literally hungry, Kane went over to the concession stand to buy some chips but ended up hearing someone dribbling in the auxiliary gym. Kane let his curiosity lead him into that gym.[iv] The kid dribbling the ball was Ja Morant.

The reason why Morant was in the auxiliary gym was that he was a late entry to the combine and was not supposed to be in Spartanburg at all. No one in the country knew his name because he was not highly recruited. But when Kane saw him playing three-on-three, he noticed the deceptive athleticism and the smooth handles that the skinny guard possessed.

Kane's curiosity led him to introduce himself to Tee Morant, who was filming what his son was doing. He quickly asked for Tee's number and told him that he was going to come back the following day so that he could watch the younger Morant play five-on-five. And when he saw Ja scoring 30 points in a five-on-five game, he was so in disbelief that no one was high on this kid. That disbelief soon transformed into a sense of urgency for the assistant coach.

Kane quickly called Murray head coach Matt McMahon to tell him to get himself over to Spartanburg as quickly as possible because he believed that despite no other scout being able to see his talent, Ja Morant was going to be a pro someday.

"Right away you saw the athleticism, the creativity, the playmaking skills, and then the edge he plays with," said MacMahon, who had to drive three hours from Atlanta during a recruitment job. "The flair. You saw that right away. Went back the next weekend in Greensboro, and he averaged 40 points over the four games. And at that point you're just hoping you can find a way to get him."[v]

It was after that game in Greensboro that McMahon offered a scholarship to Morant. From then on, the entire recruitment program focused heavily on the young man because they did not want any other school to notice him and try to pluck him away from them. McMahon and his coaches tried everything when they were selling Murray to the Morant family. One of the things that the coaches told Morant was that he could become a pro because they have a history of point guards getting picked in the top 35 of the draft. Of course, they also sold the fact that Murray State is located in a small town, which fit what Morant had been accustomed to at that point in his life. And Ja loved being in a tight-knit community.

But what at last had Ja and his family listening was the fact that Murray State wanted the young man. As a young player trying to make his way up the ladder, all he desired was to be wanted by a team. And yet he was ignored by the bigger programs. But here was Murray State making him feel the love that he did not receive from the other schools. As Ja himself said, "Murray State made me a priority".[v]

During a visit to Murray State, Ja and his family had dinner in McMahon's house. Tee told the coach that his son needed to take a break in the restroom because he was not feeling well. A distressed McMahon furiously tried to do what he could to make the player feel comfortable the moment he left the restroom because all he wanted to do was to convince Ja to play for him.

When Morant left the restroom, he pulled a fast one on the coach because he was wearing a Murray State shirt. Meanwhile, Tee put a Murray State hat on his head as Ja told McMahon, "I'm ready." That was the story of how Morant made the decision to join Murray State and effectively shut down his recruitment. It was an intimate affair that happened behind closed doors, but Morant probably preferred it that way.

As Morant left high school, he was not ranked by any of the major recruiting services in the country. Names like *ESPN* and *Rivals* thought that he was not even good enough to crack the top 100 players in the country. But it did not matter because he was going to a place he wanted to be. All he wanted was for the program to want him. And when a player is wanted, that makes an entire world of differences in someone's self-esteem and confidence.

Chapter 3: College Career

Freshman Season

Ja Morant joined an unheralded Murray State team that did not see a lot of attention from NBA scouts due to a smaller conference that did not have the most competitive programs. On top of that, Murray State was never known for producing the best players in the NBA. Not a lot of top-rated high school players went to Murray State because it was not the best in terms of its overall funding and competitiveness. Morant, however, more concerned about the program wanting him, did not care where he was going. He was an unheralded point guard that did not see many offers from different programs. And while he may have earned some offers during his senior year because of his height and athleticism at the playmaking position, he still stuck with the decision to go to Murray State. With Morant, whose confidence grew from the fact that he felt wanted, he might not have attracted much attention from scouts during his high school career, but he soon proved to be a future star.

As a freshman, Morant was already good enough to play the starting point guard position, a role he was promised before he decided to go to Murray State. He already had McMahon's trust, and he made him the focus of his recruitment. And because McMahon trusted Morant, he was willing to give the starting point guard spot to a player that other coaches all over the country were not even willing to offer a scholarship to.

Averaging 27 points in high school, Morant continued to improve on the offensive end during his freshman year in college. However, his ability to make plays was already good enough for someone who deserved a starting point guard spot in college. At a time when point guards in the NBA were focused more on their ability to score, Morant was a true point guard in every sense of the word because he could make plays for others and would rather pass to his teammates than score the ball.

It was clear that Morant was born to run the offense when he dished out 11 assists during his college debut game against Brescia. And while he was never the best scorer during his freshman year in college, he went on to score 16 points against Middle Tennessee.

The first time that Morant had a double-double in college was when he scored 10 points and grabbed 12 rebounds against Saint Louis on December 12, 2017. After that, against Marist, he finished with 16 points and ten assists. This was only a glimpse of what Morant could do whenever he was given the freedom to do whatever he wanted with the ball.

Against Detroit on December 22, Morant went on to have 17 points, 11 rebounds, and nine assists in what was nearly a triple-double effort for him. One game later, he made his best Russell Westbrook impression when he finished a win over Eastern Illinois with 11 points, ten rebounds, and 14 assists. That was his first career triple-double in college.

While he was not known as a scorer in his freshman year in college, Morant showcased his growing offensive package from January to February of 2018. He averaged 15.3 points, eight rebounds, and 6.4 assists in a seven-game span that saw him scoring double digit points in each game. In one of those games, he scored a new career-high of 23 points while making 8 of his 12 field goals in a win over Southeast Missouri State.

Thanks to his efforts as arguably the best player for Murray State, the program was able to win the Ohio Valley Conference championship. This allowed the Murray State Racers to make it to the NCAA Tournament, wherein they lost in the first round. Still, Morant scored 14 in his first-ever appearance in the NCAA Tournament, as he gained attention from scouts and coaches all over the country due to his efforts.

As a freshman, Morant averaged 12.7 points, 6.5 rebounds, and 6.3 assists. Due to his amazing performances as a freshman, he was able to earn the first-team All-OVC and OVC All-Newcomer Team awards. The sky was the limit for the rising star, who was turning 19 years old. He was young and full of potential as a 6'3" guard that was looking to take the entire nation by storm.

Sophomore Season

After Morant's freshman season in college, Jonathan Stark and Terrell Miller, the team's leading scorers, were graduating and needed to leave control over the team to the point guard that was arguably the team's best player during the 2017-18 season. And with Morant leading the way, Murray State suddenly became a threat.

Of course, the only reason why Murray State was doing any damage was due to the fact that Morant was playing at an insane level as a sophomore. Not many players of his caliber stayed for more than a year in college. But because Morant was playing on a smaller team in a less competitive conference, he needed at least a year more to prove that he was ready to make it to the NBA..

During his sophomore year, the entire nation was fixated on the arrival of Zion Williamson, Ja Morant's former AAU teammate. The basketball world wanted to know what Zion was capable of, and that was why Duke was the most-watched team during the 2018-19 college season. While Williamson was already receiving accolades as the best player in college and the consensus top overall pick in the 2019 NBA Draft, a certain lanky point guard from Murray State was making his way up the ladder while increasing his draft stock.

In just his season debut in his sophomore year, Morant had already surpassed expectations, especially after being one of the point guards invited into Chris Paul's

Elite Guard Camp. Against Wright State, he finished with 26 points and 11 assists, as he already performed better than he ever did during his freshman year. And this was far from his best performance.

Against Missouri State, Morant went for his second career triple-double in college by going for 29 points, 13 rebounds, and 12 assists. He also made six of the 12 three-pointers he shot, as his jump shot used to be his biggest weakness. And while he did have ten turnovers against Alabama on November 26, 2018, Morant was able to score a new career-high of 38 points.

He continued his run of amazing performances when he had seven straight games of double-doubles as a playmaking and scoring point guard. In the seven games he played from December 29, 2018, to January 19, 2019, he averaged 26.1 points and 12.7 assists. In a win over Eastern Kentucky, he scored 34 points and dished out ten assists. Then one game after that, he finished with a new career-high of 18 assists against

UT-Martin. Morant ended that amazing seven-game run with a new career-high of 40 points, 11 assists, and five steals against SIU-Edwardsville.

Morant became a national sensation. Even though Zion was the talk of the town and was the consensus top overall pick for 2019, Morant quickly showcased his overall abilities as a performer. He could score, make plays for others, rebound the ball, and defend. He could do it all, and that was something no one would ever expect from an unranked point guard. Morant was practically flying all over the court while showcasing his amazing leaping ability on both offense and defense.

Even though the nation had been drooling over Williamson's ability to throw the ball down, Morant was also putting down his own poster dunks. In that aforementioned 18-assist game against UT-Martin, he managed to jump over a 6'8" player to throw the ball down. It was shades of Vince Carter jumping over a

French seven-footer for a dunk back in the 2000 Olympics. And that amazing throwdown was the one proof anyone needed to see when it came down to Morant's ability to jump. As his mother always reminded him in high school, he was beneath no one in that play.

By January 2019, Morant was on everyone's radar. He was a national sensation that teams in the NBA wanted a piece of in the upcoming draft. Scouts and analysts alike were already saying that he was going to be the next player who was going to be chosen in the top five coming out of a mid-major college team. This meant a great deal to Morant, who had been an unheralded player coming out of high school. But now, everyone in the nation knew his name as one of the top five players vying for an NBA draft spot in 2019.

His meteoric rise to the top was not something that resulted from mere maturity, growth, and athletic development, however. Morant worked hard to get to where he was. He was always seen as a hard worker that was always relentless in his approach as a basketball player. No matter how great he performed on the court, he always found a way to get better, having been raised to believe that he was never going to be good enough. He even went on to say that, no matter how well he performed in college, his father never told him he was great. This allowed him to stay hungry.[iii]

A good example of how relentless Morant was in his approach to get better was that he never took any days off. Whenever he had the opportunity to work on his game or play a pick-up game, he always did so. After losing in the 2018 National Tournament, he found a way to play a pick-up game. And during a 48-hour Christmas break in 2018, he found time to play ball instead of resting. This was the relentless approach that he possessed.

Of course, Morant also found ways to work on his weaknesses. It was not common for college players to rely more on their dominant hand whenever they were making passes. But Morant, who was more accustomed to using one hand when passing the ball, learned how to make passes using his left hand so that he could still make plays for his teammates when defenses were looking to take away his right-hand passing lanes. "He had multiple games where he had more assists passing with his left hand than his right," McMahon said.[v]

Seen as a Russell Westbrook clone, Morant was someone the defense would rather gamble on by giving him space to shoot jump shots. They were more afraid of his ability to break defenses down with his athletic way of getting to the basket. No one wanted him to dunk on their heads in the lane, and that was why defenses would rather force him to shoot three-pointers. However, during February and March, he was making 45% of his three-point shots. This meant that Morant was working on his weaknesses instead of resting on his laurels. While some of the other college players would try to focus more on their strengths, the Murray State star point guard never thought that he was enough. This allowed him to find ways to improve, especially on his perceived weaknesses, which included his jump shot. Morant's improved play and all-around prowess as a complete point guard turned him into one of the deadliest collegiate stars in recent memory.

As Morant continued to tear down the collegiate ranks with his athleticism and ability to take control over an offense, he led his team to another conference championship and an appearance in the NCAA Tournament. It was in Murray State's win against Marquette in March Madness that he was able to put up 17 points, 11 rebounds, and 16 assists. He became only the eighth player in tournament history to have a triple-double. And while he scored 28 against Florida

State, the Racers dropped that one and bowed out of the NCAA Tournament.

Morant, a consensus All-American, averaged 24.5 points, 5.7 rebounds, and ten assists. He led the entire nation in assists, as the next one closest to his number averaged only 7.7 dimes per game. Of course, Ja Morant also became the first person in the history of the NCAA to average 20 points and ten assists in a single season. There have been plenty of great players that have come and gone from the collegiate ranks, some able to score 30 points in a heartbeat, while others could dish dimes quite easily. But none of them were able to achieve what Morant did in his sophomore season. He was truly beneath no one.[vi]

Ja Morant was now a national sensation just two years after not even being ranked nationally. But after Morant's dominant sophomore season in college, the 19-year old phenom was on his way to greatness in the NBA. This time, unlike what happened in 2017 when he was unranked and underrecruited, no team was going to pass out on him. He had truly come a long way from the last-minute addition that James Kane discovered in the Spartanburg Day auxiliary gym in 2016.

Chapter 4: NBA Career

Getting Drafted

The 2019 NBA Draft was set to become one of the deepest in recent history because of how it presented many different players that were talented in their own right. Of course, the headliner of the draft was the Duke standout, Zion Williamson, who won all of the college Player of the Year awards as a freshman. And because Williamson was touted as a rare talent that had the size, athleticism, and skill not seen from most players, the entire draft was focused on him.

Even though the draft lottery was basically the Zion Williamson sweepstakes, as the New Orleans Pelicans were dead-set on drafting the young man with the top overall pick, Morant had also made a name for himself in college. He was already used to getting overlooked because no one in high school ever thought he would become good enough for college. But this time, he was the next best player behind Williamson.

Unlike many prospects that made their way to the NBA, the numbers told the entire story of how good Ja Morant was in college. He averaged 24.5 points and ten assists in his final college season to become the first and only player in NCAA history to average at least 20 points and ten assists in a single season. And those numbers were not merely the product of a good player playing for a small team, as Morant also passed the eye test as well.

The one things that stood out for anyone observing Morant were his physical tools as an athlete. Reaching a height of 6'3" after spending much of his younger years as a shorter point guard, he had the right size to contend with the likes of Russell Westbrook, Kyrie Irving, and Stephen Curry in the NBA. His height allowed him to see over the top of defenses when making plays. He could also use his long arms to make passes and score over the top of defenses. But the one standout physical was his leaping ability. His athletic skills were not headlining the news websites and social media during his sophomore season because Zion Williamson was the nation's highlight machine by default. However, Morant could jump out of the building with his explosive leaping ability, reaching heights that could clear a 6'8" player with ease. Plenty of his highlights in college were of him dunking on top of centers and even using both hands to block shots and pin the ball on the backboard.

The Russell Westbrook comparisons were obvious because Ja Morant possessed the same nuclear leaping ability and explosive athleticism. He was also like Westbrook in the sense that he possessed the ability to do it all on the floor, as evidenced by his many triple-doubles in college. But the most surprising part about Morant's game was the fact that he could be more refined than Westbrook.

Throughout his entire career, Russell Westbrook was seen as a hardnosed player that had all of the heart and athleticism in the world but was too fast and too athletic for his own basketball IQ and skills to keep up. Westbrook went after every rebound and found a way to make plays for his teammates, but lacked the refined jumper that point guards should have. On top of that, he also struggled with his turnovers. But Ja Morant, despite being as young as he was when he was entering the NBA draft, already had the makings of a player that could possibly become more refined. It might be true that he did not possess the same speed that Westbrook had in his prime, but Morant played a more controlled style of basketball. And when defenses dared to take away his ability to get to the basket and dunk over defenders, he could drain jump shots off the dribble.

On offense, he had everything that a scoring point guard needed. Morant knew how to use his athleticism to finish with strong layups or dunks, yet could also stop on a dime in the paint and finish against strong inside defenders using his floater. And while his jump shot was still a work in progress, he had shown the ability to hit them consistently.

In a way, Morant was supposed to be the next evolution of the Westbrook prototype. He was fast, athletic, and always seemingly hungry. However, he came with a more refined skill package that blended well with his ability to change his pace and pick his spots out on the floor, whether he was looking for his own shots or making plays for his teammates. And he was just as aggressive on offense as any point guard in college. He never took any plays off and was relentless at attacking the opposing defenses as a scorer or playmaker.

Speaking of his playmaking, there was nothing bad that could be said about Morant's ability to make plays for others. College players averaging ten assists a game was something that almost never happened. In 2018, Trae Young came close while he was leading the nation in scoring and assists. However, he fell a few assists shy of averaging ten assists. Morant, on the other hand, possessed the height, speed, and length that made him arguably a more promising player than Young, despite his being a great playmaker himself.

One of the most amazing parts about Ja Morant's passing was that he was more comfortable making passes with one hand than he was with two hands. The reason was that he wanted to master the art of making passes quickly with one hand after the dribble because these passes were faster to pull off and more difficult for defenders to anticipate. And Morant even mastered the art of making these one-handed passes with his left hand. As such, because of his ability to make quick passes with one hand while dribbling the ball, he led the entire nation in transition points.[vii] He was at his most dangerous after rebounding the ball because he could quickly put it on the floor and zoom over to the other end for a quick bucket. The open floor was his comfort zone. And with the NBA transitioning more to an open and fast-paced game, Morant could easily make the transition from college to pro in that aspect.

Morant was also a terrific rebounder at the point guard spot in college, having averaged five to six rebounds in his two years with Murray State. This means that he was active at getting to the ball and was great at using his athleticism to jump over any player to grab the rebound. And when Morant was rebounding the ball, there was a good chance that he was going to take the ball over to the other end for a slam or a great pass to a streaking teammate.

The offensive outlook on Morant was mostly positive because he could be expected to do everything on offense. He could score in both the half-court and on transition because of his refined skills and ability to finish in the basket. The jump shot was a work in progress, but it was a growing part of his game. On top of that, he could make plays at a high level.

As good as Morant may have been, there were still concerns about his overall game, especially concerning his glaring weaknesses. And a lot of his weaknesses stemmed from the fact that he always had a slight frame that made him look very thin and weak, even for a point guard standing at 6'3".

Unlike the likes of Russell Westbrook and Derrick Rose, who were already physical specimens when they got to the NBA, Morant was always skinny. This became a huge drawback in his game because he could not always power his way through defenders that became overtly physical with him. And while he possessed the hops that allowed him to finish over paint defenders, he tended to struggle against the bigger and more athletic rim protectors in the NBA.

On the defensive end, Morant was capable of showing his ability to pressure the ball handler with his long arms and amazing mobility. However, he was usually quite lazy on defense, especially when playing off the ball or when chasing his defensive assignment around the floor. He easily got picked off on screens and was already willing to give up whenever he was screened from his defensive assignment. A bit more weight and effort could be a good way of improving his defensive skills in the NBA. The tools were already there, but he only needed to become more refined as a defender.

Morant's jump shot was also a work in progress when he was still making his way to the NBA. He was not a bad shooter because he was shooting somewhere close to 34% in college. In fact, in his final games during February and March, he shot over 40% from the three-point line. All he needed was a bit more consistency to get to become a star in the NBA because defenders could always dare him to shoot the jump shot instead of gambling on his ability to break defenses down with his slashing and playmaking.

There were even more things Morant needed to improve on. In college, his assists came off drive-and-dish situations and transition opportunities. He struggled to make plays during pick-and-roll situations, but that could have been a product of playing alongside players that were not adept at setting screens or scoring off the pick-and-roll. Morant could possibly improve in this aspect playing alongside a professional pick-and-roll player in the NBA.

Like Russell Westbrook, there were also instances when Morant looked somewhat loose when handling the ball. This led to costly turnovers on his part, especially when he was moving faster than his basketball IQ allowed him to do. But that was merely part of being a young point guard still learning more about the game and how to handle different types of defensive looks. Experience and training in the next level could make him into a better decision-making point guard that was more in control over the ball than in college.

There was also the fact that Morant, while putting in impressive numbers, was playing for a mid-major program that did not see a lot of tough competitors in its conference. Had he played for bigger programs that played in tougher conferences, the story would perhaps have been different as far as his stats were concerned. But the concern now was whether or not he could play against professional teams that were far better than the competition he faced in college.

Still, the outlook for Morant was mostly positive. He did not even work out for any team or join the Draft Combine because his stock was already at an all-time high. He had nothing to prove for the NBA teams that were willing to draft him. All he had was his resume and the things that scouts raved about him during his two years with Murray State. All that said, Morant was a shoo-in for one of the top three spots in the 2019 NBA Draft. The outlook was for him to go second or third because the top overall spot was already going to Zion Williamson. However, there was a good reason to believe that he was going to get chosen second overall because the Memphis Grizzlies were in dire need of a younger point guard.

Prior to the 2019-20 season, the Grizzlies spent a good part of the 2010s working on a grit-and-grind offense that broke the mold in a league that was fueled by fast-paced offenses and three-point shots. They relied on the steady presence of former franchise point guard Mike Conley, who they drafted back in 2007. Conley was the perfect point guard for the slow-paced offense because he knew how to pace himself and make the best decisions for a team that tried to grind every possession out. However, the Grizzlies realized that they needed to move on from that era when their frontline duo of Marc Gasol and Zach Randolph was getting older. While Conley was still capable of leading an offense from the backcourt, the Grizzlies wanted to rebuild from the ground. Drafting a newer and fresher point guard was the perfect way to rebuild because the Grizzlies could build a team around a new franchise playmaker.

And so, during draft night, the New Orleans Pelicans made the most obvious choice by drafting Zion Williamson out of Duke. Considering that they needed the next best player and a new point guard to lead their offense, the Memphis Grizzlies drafted Ja Morant with the second overall pick. He was now the new franchise point guard for the Grizzlies, as Memphis eventually traded Mike Conley a few weeks after drafting the young man out of Murray State.

Two years ago, in 2017, Ja Morant left high school as an unranked player that was on nobody's radar; now he was the second overall pick and was set to become a franchise player for an NBA team—a tribute to how hard work and perseverance eventually wins out.

Rookie of the Year

When Morant was drafted by the Grizzlies, the goal of the team was to rebuild around him. The Grizzlies already had talented big man Jaren Jackson Jr., the son of former NBA player Jaren Jackson. Jackson Jr. was also ninth in Morant's recruitment class in 2017.

Building around Ja Morant allowed the Grizzlies to have some leverage when they traded former franchise point guard Mike Conley to the Utah Jazz. While they got some useful pieces in the Conley trade, the best part about it was that the Grizzlies could now play Morant full-time as their starting point guard. Entering his rookie year, he was beneath no one at the point guard spot on his team.

Prior to Morant's arrival, the Grizzlies were a grind-it-out team that focused on giving the ball to their post players while also keeping the pace of the game low. They were able to grind wins out through their slow and methodical manner of killing opponents. The Grizzlies played good hardnosed defense while making sure that the opposing team's best players were given the worst looks possible on a team that stacked the frontcourt with physical big men and the backcourt with elite perimeter defenders. Despite the fact that the Grizzlies were unable to win a title during what they call the "grindhouse era," they competed well enough during the regular season and in the playoffs, as they were able to give elite teams like the San Antonio Spurs and the Golden State Warriors a good run for their money. But as key pieces like Marc Gasol, Zack Randolph, and Tony Allen were already too old, it was time for the Grizzlies to rebuild.

The logical solution was to build around a point guard like Morant. That was because the modern NBA during the time when Morant was drafted was focused on guard and perimeter play. Almost all of the teams had point guards that were capable of scoring the ball and making plays for their teammates at stellar levels. Of course, drafting Morant meant that the Grizzlies needed to change their identity as well.

It was clear that the slow-paced style that the Grizzlies used to favor during the grindhouse era was not going to fit the speed and athleticism of Morant and the young legs of the other players they were looking to use as their building blocks for the future. As such, the Grizzlies, under new head coach Taylor Jenkins, were now looking to speed things up and change the entire culture of the franchise. It was now the Ja Morant era in Memphis.

The moment that Morant joined the Grizzlies, it was clear that he was going to have the ball in his hands a lot. Memphis did not have a lot of veteran stars that needed the ball to be effective. In fact, during the 2019-20 season, the oldest starter on the team was Jae Crowder, who did not last long because he was traded in the middle of the campaign. This allowed Morant to have full control over the offense.

In his first game as a professional, Morant scored 14 points in a loss to the Miami Heat. However, it did not take too long for his offense to pick up in the NBA and adjust to the more physical brand of basketball of the professional league. In a win over the Brooklyn Nets on October 27, 2019, he finished with 30 points and nine assists. It was about to become clear that he was going to be a star in the league.

Against Phoenix, Houston, and Minnesota in a three-game stretch, Morant finished with three straight games of 20 or more points while shooting a good clip from the floor. Then, on November 13, he went for his first NBA double-double performance when he finished with 23 points and 11 assists. He was playing beyond his age because he could both score and make plays for others. In back-to-back losses to the Indiana Pacers and the Los Angeles Clippers late in November, he finished with two straight double-double performances.

While anyone could say a lot of things about Morant's brilliance during the early part of his rookie year, what people noticed more was his fearlessness. As a highlight-reel machine in college, he continued his high-flying ways in the NBA by dunking in the lane whenever possible and by attacking rim protectors with awesome dunk attempts. And even when he was missing his dunks, the crowd loved the fact that he was more than willing to throw the ball down on the heads of big men whenever possible.

It was Morant's fearlessness and aggressive mentality that made him better than advertised when he was entering college. And thanks to the confidence he gained when he was the man over at Murray State, Morant's belief in his abilities was at an all-time high when he entered the NBA. He was not afraid of anyone because he had no reason to be afraid.

The Grizzlies, meanwhile, started 6-14 through their first 20 games during the 2019-20 season. This was something that they expected because the franchise was still rebuilding. Then again, thanks to Morant's efforts, the Grizzlies were able to look competitive during the middle portion of the regular season. From January 4 to 17, 2020, they went on a seven-game stretch of consecutive wins. Throughout that span of games, Morant had All-Star numbers of 19.3 points, five rebounds, and nine assists while shooting 59% from the floor.

In January of 2020, the Grizzlies were trending in the right direction because they only lost four games during that time. And Morant scored in single digits only once during the entire calendar month, all while averaging great rookie numbers of 17.5 points and 8.3 assists during January. Then, in what seemed to be the best game he had played at that point in his career, he had his first career triple-double of 27 points, ten rebounds, and ten assists in a win over the Washington Wizards on February 9. Then on February 29, he finished a win over the Los Angeles Lakers, the eventual champions that season, with 27 points and a career-high of 14 assists.

Morant's rookie season had to be put on hold when the NBA had to suspend the 2019-20 season. Late in 2019, a new Coronavirus was discovered in Wuhan, China. Dubbed COVID-19. The virus made its way across the rest of the world a few months in 2020. When the Utah Jazz's Rudy Gobert became the first person to test positive for the virus, the NBA had to suspend the season indefinitely.[viii]

As the NBA was still trying to find a way around the virus during the quarantine period, Morant made the most out of the time that he was away from the game. No team was allowed to meet up together during the suspension of the season, and that meant that the players had to train on their own while finding ways to stay in shape. That was exactly what Ja Morant did during the near-four-month hiatus of the NBA.

While in quarantine in his home, Morant tried his best to stay in shape by working out on his own. On top of that, he also tried to find ways to pack some muscle.

After all, his body frame had always been his weakness when he got to the NBA. He might have had the vertical leaping ability and the speed of a capable guard, but the problem was that he could not always rely on his athleticism to score on top of defenders. Of course, on defense, he struggled to fight his way through screens. And so, he trained using weights while also eating healthy meals that allowed him to pack some muscle. He tried to gain weight during the NBA's hiatus, eventually packing on 12 pounds of pure muscle. This was good news for the Grizzlies, as their franchise player was willing to put in the work to become better, all while some of the other players in the league used the time off to rest.

"I'll be able to absorb contact, be able to use my body more," Morant said. "Getting through different screens. That's just what I'm looking to be able to do when we get to Orlando. The things I've been doing before, but better."[ix]

Even after putting on muscle, Morant said that he was able to improve his athleticism. A lot of the muscle and strength he gained went to his legs, as his vertical leaping continued to improve.

"You know I think that's a huge credit to the work he's been putting in over the last couple of months and obviously gaining strength has been a priority of his and being able to maintain his supreme athleticism," head coach Taylor Jenkins said with pride.[x]

As the NBA officials met with the team owners and the representatives of the NBPA, a compromise was settled. The stakeholders decided to resume the season in the final week of July 2020 but in a "bubble" format that was going to be held in Orlando, Florida. Only the teams that were seven wins away from the eighth spot of their respective conferences were invited to play in the Orlando bubble. And thanks to the surge that the Grizzlies had in the middle portion of the regular season, they were on the list.

Unfortunately for the Grizzlies, they could not muster enough wins in the bubble to make it to the playoffs. But the good news was that Morant continued to show out while also showcasing his improved physical capabilities. He finished the bubble games with three straight double-double performances. And in the final game against the Milwaukee Bucks on August 13, he finished with 12 points, ten assists, and a new career-high of 13 rebounds.

During the bubble games in Orlando, Morant averaged 18.6 points, 6.4 rebounds, and 9.7 assists. He may have struggled with his shot, which was acceptable due to the long hiatus, but he showcased his improved strength and growing athletic skills in those seven games.

In his rookie year, Morant averaged 17.8 points, 3.9 rebounds, and 7.3 assists while shooting a great clip of 47.7% from the field. The Grizzlies, even though they were not expected to achieve a lot that season, won a total of 34 games in the first year of the Morant era. It was clear that the future was bright for the team.

Even though his rookie season was over, there were more things for Morant to achieve in his first year in the NBA. That was because he was one of the three finalists for the NBA Rookie of the Year. The other finalists were Kendrick and Zion Williamson. Meanwhile, Brandon Clarke, another surprisingly good rookie for the Grizzlies, nearly became a finalist.

The case for Ja Morant as the Rookie of the Year was obvious. Among all of the rookies that season, he was the most consistent in terms of his performance and health. He was available in all but six of the 73 games that the Grizzlies played during the 2019-20 regular season. And he was also putting up considerably good numbers for a rookie while also showcasing the fearlessness and athleticism that made him a household name during his sophomore year in college.

Meanwhile, Kendrick Nunn was also making a good case for the award because he was a surprisingly good rookie, even though he was undrafted coming out of college. He could score exceptionally well and was capable of manning the point guard position for a Miami Heat that overachieved that season. And he contributed well on one of the most balanced offensive teams in the NBA, all while showcasing that he belonged in the league.

Then there was Zion Williamson, the man who took the nation by storm in his lone season in Duke. Zion missed several games that season because of an injury he suffered before the regular season began. He appeared in only 24 games during the 2019-20 regular season but showcased the talent and raw athletic skills that made him a prodigy. Averaging 22.5 points and 6.3 rebounds while shooting 58.3% from the field in only 28 minutes a game, he was frighteningly efficient. But then again, Zion only played in 24 games, which were quite enough for the voters to vote him as a finalist.

In the end, the eventual winner of the Rookie of the Year award was Ja Morant, who finished with a nearly unanimous 99 out of 100 first-place votes. The last person to win the award unanimously was Karl-Anthony Towns back in 2016, and only five players in history had won unanimously. Morant was one vote away from becoming the sixth.

While there were people who believed that he only became Rookie of the Year because Zion was injured, the fact of the matter was that Morant was there to put on great numbers for a rookie night in and night out. The best skills that an NBA player can have are his availability and the ability to stay healthy, and Morant was always available to play for his team whenever he could.

Morant's success could be credited to his confidence and an undying will to work harder than anyone else.

But his job was far from done, as he was still looking to work harder than ever to become one of the brightest young stars in the entire league. And no one ever thought that he would rise through the ranks so quickly.

First Playoff Year

After his successful Rookie of the Year campaign, Morant focused more on strengthening his body and making sure that he gained enough weight to handle the physical grind of playing against bigger and stronger defenders in the NBA, as he was about to enter his second year in the NBA.

It was during the 2020-21 NBA season that the league had one of the shortest offseasons. The league concluded on October 11, 2020, when the Los Angeles Lakers won the championship. Meanwhile, the 2020-21 season was set to begin right around Christmas of the same year. This meant that Morant and the other incoming second-year players only had a few months to prepare.

Due to the rare circumstances surrounding the league, which was going to proceed without fans during the earlier portion of the regular season, the NBA decided to shake things up a bit. The seventh and eighth teams of each conference would fight for the right for the seventh seed in the playoffs. Meanwhile, the loser of that game would have to battle the ninth-placed team for the final spot in the playoffs. This rule eventually became beneficial for the Grizzlies.

Morant did not take long to show out in his first game as a second-year player in the NBA. Showcasing his improved strength, he was unstoppable against the San Antonio Spurs on December 23, 2020, when he made 18 of his 27 shots to score a new career-high of 44 points. But his one-man show was not enough to give his team the win.

After a minor injury against the Atlanta Hawks in only his third game of the season, Morant missed eight straight games. But when he returned, he went on to showcase his improved skills when he led the Grizzlies to seven straight wins. He also went on an 18-game run of scoring in double digits, as Morant was now becoming more consistent as a scorer. During that run, he averaged 17.8 points and 7.9 assists. His highlight performance during that run was when he had a triple-double of 15 points, 11 rebounds, and 12 assists in a win over the Oklahoma City Thunder on February 17, 2021.

On March 2, Morant had another amazing game when he led a win over the Washington Wizards and Russell Westbrook, the very same player he looked up to when he was in high school. He outplayed his idol when he scored 35 points and dished out ten assists in that win over the Wizards. And while he lost the next game against the Milwaukee Bucks, Morant scored 30 or more points in consecutive games for the first time when he had 35 points in that outing. On March 26, Morant had another 30-point double-double performance against the Utah Jazz and Mike Conley, the very same player who was in his position as the Grizzlies' franchise point guard just a few years ago. In that game, he finished with 32 points and 11 assists. And against the very same team five days later, he finished with 36 points.

During the month of March 2021, Morant was playing at a stellar level, averaging 21.1 points and 7.1 assists in that run. On top of that, he scored 30 or more points in four games during that month. And he was only getting better. as the Grizzlies' hopes for a playoff berth were becoming more and more apparent. On April 5, he scored 37 points and finished with ten assists in a win over the Minnesota Timberwolves. And his efforts during the final portion of the regular season were more than enough to give the Grizzlies life as the ninth-place team in the Western Conference.

When the Golden State Warriors lost the right to the seventh seed on a buzzer-beating shot from LeBron James, they needed to battle the Memphis Grizzlies for the eighth spot in the West. This became the battle between the present and the future, as Morant was up against Stephen Curry.

At this point in the NBA, there was no arguing against the fact that Curry was the best point guard in the league, at the level of the greatest players in the entire professional ranks. Widely regarded as one of the best point guards in history, perhaps just as good as Magic Johnson, who is often called the greatest player to ever play the position, and also the greatest shooter the game of basketball has ever seen. This was the man who led the NBA in scoring during the 2020-21 season and scored 50 or more points multiple times on his way to his second scoring title. Curry was also one of the three finalists for the MVP award that season and was looking to add a third MVP to the two that he already had. And, of course, he was a three-time NBA champion at that point in time. In a way, Ja Morant was looking at the man who owned the point guard position in the NBA and was the player responsible for changing basketball into the run-and-gun and shooting game that it is today. Curry's accolades were light-years ahead of what Morant had accomplished at that point in his career. And despite that, Morant was not intimidated by one of the greatest players the game of basketball has ever seen. True to his fearless nature, he kept coming at the Warriors in that play-in game for the final spot of the playoffs.

Morant and the Grizzlies fought the gritty Warriors to an overtime affair. And when it was time for Morant to show up, he hit the go-ahead floater to seal the deal for Memphis in that amazing game against Curry and the Warriors, finishing with 35 points while delivering Memphis a playoff spot for the first time in the Ja Morant era. That game against the Warriors was a glimpse of the future of the point guard spot, as Morant battled it out with the best point guard in the

NBA and ended up winning the bout. Even though Curry is still considered the best point guard in the league, Morant has been steadily climbing to the top of the list as one of the greatest young stars in the NBA at his position.

During the 2020-21 regular season, Morant finished with averages of 19.1 points, four rebounds, and 7.4 assists. He was not yet playing at a level of an All-Star, but he was surely getting there. And the most important part of that season for him was that the Grizzlies were able to make it to the playoffs via the play-in tournament that was in its inaugural season.

Ja Morant put in the required work against the Utah Jazz in the playoffs, as this was a team that he performed well against during the regular season. But the problem was that, at that point in his career, he was a one-man show against a complete and well-rounded Jazz team that won the top seed in the West. Still, that did not faze him one bit.

The Grizzlies shocked the Utah Jazz in Game 1 when they took the win. In Morant's first-ever playoff game, he scored 26 points. But that ultimately became his first and only playoff win at that point in his career because the Jazz showed why they won the top seed in the West. In Game 2, Morant had a valiant effort that allowed him to play the best game he has ever played in his entire career. He attacked the basket fearlessly, even with Rudy Gobert, the NBA's Defensive Player of the Year that season, manning the paint. Morant did not care who was in front of him because he was attacking relentlessly on his way to his best scoring performance of 47 points.

Despite Morant's efforts, the Grizzlies lost to a more balanced team that had more scorers and contributors. The Jazz, after losing Game 1, went on to win four straight games to kick the Grizzlies out of the postseason. And throughout all of the five games that the Grizzlies played in the playoffs, Morant was brilliant, as he averaged 30.2 points n 48.7% from the floor against the Jazz's tough defense.

Even though the Grizzlies could not make it out of the first round, the future was bright for them because of Morant. His performance during the playoffs was an indication of better things to come for him and his team. And no one expected that he would be able to quickly rise to the level of an All-Star or even an MVP candidate in only his third year in the NBA.

The All-Star Starter

After two years of playing in the NBA, Morant was already a crowd favorite all over the globe. He was not putting up amazing numbers that deserved an All-Star spot, but everyone in the world loved the fact that he looked like a star on the rise. Morant was not afraid to attack the basket and perform vicious dunks that probably became posters on every Memphis kid's wall. And he was also known as the league's best "what if" dunker because of the many different dunks that he missed after literally jumping over his defenders.

But at that point, the consensus regarding Morant was that he was a ridiculous athlete that still needed to work on the finer aspects of his game. He could jump out of the building and finish at the rim with ease, as evidenced by the fact that he made more than 60% of all of his baskets within three feet away from the basket during his first two years. However, he lacked the jump shot and the other finesse parts that could help turn him into one of the most dangerous point guards in the league.

Others thought that what Morant needed was to work on his strength. Point guards are expected to make their jump shots, but that should not be where their game should revolve around. Not anyone can be Stephen Curry or Damian Lillard, arguably the two most dangerous shooters at the point guard position. And not every point guard should perform the razzle-dazzle moves and hit the contested jump shots that Kyrie Irving was known for. In that regard, Morant only needed to stay true to himself. He needed to work on his strengths more while also minimizing his weaknesses as much as possible. There was still no need for him to develop the in-between jump shot that Chris Paul was known for. But it was imperative for him to become a respectable outside threat and a better finisher in the paint if he wanted to keep his defenders on their heels. And that was what Morant did during the offseason when he became stronger, healthier, and more refined.

The work that Morant put himself through during the offseason was more than enough for him to take his game to the next level. He did not have to change his identity because he was already a fantastic player. All he needed to do was to keep working on what he did best while also becoming a better decision-making point guard, regardless of whether he was going to score the basket or make plays for his teammates. And the maturity and experience he gained through his first two seasons were what he needed to put the entire league on notice that he was coming in fast and strong.

Morant was nothing short of sensational during the early part of the 2021-22 season. He started the regular season with a fantastic performance of 37 points against the Cleveland Cavaliers on October 20, 2021. Just four days later, he put up 40 points in a loss to the Los Angeles Lakers. And he continued to be relentless for Memphis by scoring 30 or more points six times during his first 18 games. This was a season wherein players were adjusting in the early part because of certain rule changes that prevented the offensive player from drawing fouls by initiating contact with the defender. On top of that, there were also players that were adjusting to the new balls provided by a new company. But Morant, whose game was never predicated on his ability to fish fouls or his jump shot did not care about all that. He could draw fouls extremely well and could hit the jump shot whenever he needed to. But his game did not rely on either of those. Instead, he was more likely to try to get to the point using his speed and explosiveness and finish near the rim with his amazing leaping ability and soft touch in the paint. And all of those were highlighted during the early portion of the season when he averaged 25.3 points, 5.8 rebounds, and 7.1 assists through his first 18 games.

But his quick start to the season was temporarily placed on hold when he suffered a knee sprain during a loss to the Atlanta Hawks on November 26. Despite not being in the lineup for 12 straight games, Morant did not look like he was the sole reason why the Grizzlies were performing well that season. The Grizzlies looked like a well-rounded team even without their best player, as they won 10 of the 12 games that Morant missed. And not having Morant only made the rest of the Grizzlies more confident in their abilities.

When he returned to the lineup after a 12-game absence, Morant quickly dispelled the notion that the Grizzlies were better without him when he led his team to an amazing 10-game win streak. Of course, Morant was the driver of that streak, as he averaged 26.7 points, 6.4 rebounds, and 6.7 assists while shooting over 50% during that run.

Of course, as he got healthier and more confident in his game, Morant entered a mode that made people realize that he was not only a rising star but was already close to the superstar level. From January 19 to 31, 2022, he had a seven-game run of scoring 30 or more points. This run included a 41-point outburst in a win over the San Antonio Spurs. And performances like those convinced everyone that he deserved an All-Star starting spot.

"I deserve this. I earned this. I worked for this," Morant said when asked about potentially becoming an All-Star starter, "This is the way I wanted it. I didn't want to be no alternate. I don't want to be a spot-filler."[x]

The most important piece of news for Morant at that point in his life came on January 27 when the NBA announced the starters for the 2022 All-Star Game. He officially became an All-Star for the very first time in his career when he was chosen by the fans, media, and coaches as a starter. Not many players get to become All-Stars in their third season in the league. But Morant was not only an All-Star but also a starter in his very first All-Star appearance.

From a point when no major college program thought that Ja Morant was worth a scholarship offer, he quickly made all of the major programs regret passing on him back when he was in high school. And now that he was an All-Star averaging 25.8 points, 5.9 rebounds, and 6.9 assists while shooting nearly 50% from the field in only his third season, he proved that no one was beneath him.

The story behind Morant's numbers and the Grizzlies' success during that season, leading him to become an All-Star starter that belonged with the likes of LeBron James, Stephen Curry, and Nikola Jokic is more than enough to show why he was deserving of an All-Star starting spot. At first look, Morant appeared to have All-Star numbers that were quite similar to the numbers that Stephen Curry and other All-Star starting guards were putting up. But the most interesting part about his numbers was how he got them and why he was so efficient as a scorer.

During the offseason, the Memphis Grizzlies traded away starting center Jonas Valanciunas, a double-double machine, for Steven Adams, who did not put up a lot of numbers. The Adams trade proved to become beneficial for Morant, as Valanciunas could average 17 points and 12 rebounds on a nightly basis, but was more likely to fill up space in the paint because he liked playing at the low post, in addition to camping in the lane to grab rebounds. On the other hand, Adams did not put up the same gaudy numbers that Valanciunas was capable of putting up, being the type of center that excelled at setting screens at the top and allowing his guards to play the pick-and-roll effectively. And Adams did not prefer to camp in the lane due to his skill as a screener and high-post passer.

Meanwhile, the Grizzlies also saw the return of a healthy Jaren Jackson Jr. after he missed a huge chunk of the previous season due to a serious injury. Jackson Jr. was widely known as a capable jump shooter at the big man position who did not like clogging the paint on the offensive end. Moreover, during Morant's absence due to injury, other players were able to step up their game. Second-year wing Desmond Bane, the 30th pick during the 2020 NBA Draft, became a capable three-point shooter and was making more than 40% of the seven three-pointers he attempted a game. He also improved his capabilities as a scorer and went on to become a great second option for Memphis, as he averaged 18 points on a nightly basis.

Other notable role players, such as De'Anthony Melton, Kyle Anderson, Tyus Jones, and Brandon Clarke, began stepping up their games as well by contributing good scoring numbers on a regular basis. And they were also able to contribute to the Grizzlies on any kind of lineup that Taylor Jenkins fielded.

Having Steven Adams instead of Jonas Valanciunas allowed him more freedom to operate as a paint scorer because there was no one clogging the middle. Adams' superior screening ability also allowed him to play the pick-and-roll effectively. Even when the Grizzlies were not playing heavy minutes to Steven Adams whenever they played a small-ball lineup, Morant was able to operate well because he had a force of shooters around him. Jaren Jackson Jr., as a center, could hit the three-point shot. And Bane, Brooks, Melton, and Anderson spread the floor and improved the tempo to allow Morant to have the freedom he needed to do what he did well.

At the point when Morant was named an All-Star starter, he led the entire NBA in points scored in the paint by a guard. The 15.5 points he averaged in the paint are the highest that any guard has ever been able to put up in the last 25 years. One would have to go back to the time of Allen Iverson to find a guard capable of putting up points in the paint at Morant's level.

The freedom that Morant had to operate on offense allowed him to dominate as a paint scorer. In his third season, he converted more than 70% of the shots he took within three feet away from the basket. That number was at 61.8% during his first two seasons. Compared to Russell Westbrook's explosive finishing abilities, his best output at finishing within three feet from the basket stands at 65%. This proves that Morant was already at an elite level when it comes to his ability to finish near the rim.

Shot selection also improved on his part. Instead of shooting inefficient midrange shots, Morant decided to take paint shots and three-pointers instead. But the most impressive part was that he developed the in-between floater game that allowed him to score in the paint when a defender was there to protect the rim from his vicious assaults on the basket. Morant increased the volume of the shots he was taking between three and ten feet from the basket while making 43.5% of his attempts from that area.

Even though his jump shot was still a work in progress, Morant proved that he was not the type of player that defenders could just dare to shoot. He increased his three-point shot attempts while also improving his average to a respectable number of 35.4%. And there were even instances when he shot his three-pointers at distances that only Stephen Curry and Damian Lillard would dare to shoot from. Even with the increased volume of three-point attempts, Morant still averaged nearly 50% from the field for a point guard. This stems from the fact that he continued to play his role as a fearless scorer near the basket. Of course, the team that he had around him made it possible for him to play an efficient brand of basketball, especially whenever he was attacking the basket.

Morant's improved efficiency as a scorer made it possible for him to destroy defenses with his scoring and playmaking. The way he led the Grizzlies to one of the top four seeds in the West while playing at a superstar level earned him the starting spot he deserved. Arguably the only point guard better than him in the West at that point was Stephen Curry. And being second to Curry, one of the greatest of all time, is a position that any point guard would take.

Even though one could make the argument that Ja Morant was playing like he was second only to Stephen Curry, the trajectory for him was trending upward. In just his third season, he was an All-Star starter and was in the MVP conversation with the best players in the league. And it might not be too long until he eventually becomes the league's best point guard.

Chapter 5: Personal Life

Ja Morant was born and raised in Dalzell, South Carolina, although he went to school in a nearby neighborhood because his father was also a native of South Carolina, as he played alongside Ray Allen in high school. Morant stayed in South Carolina until he had to leave for college.

The eldest son in the family, he has a younger sister named Teniya, who he grew up playing basketball with in the family's backyard basketball court. Teniya currently plays basketball at the basic education level and has the chance to earn a college scholarship.

Morant lived by his mother's words of "beneath no one," and had those words tattooed on his left arm as a constant reminder.

Growing up, he idolized Russell Westbrook because of his attacking mentality and due to the fact that his idol was also often overlooked. When Morant got to college, his athleticism and the all-around game often made him the subject of comparisons to Russell Westbrook. But Ja had since been able to prove that he is an entirely unique player in his own right.

Morant also has a daughter named Kaari Jaidyn Morant, who he had with fellow athlete KK Dixon. Kaari was born in 2019, when Ja was still just starting out as a professional basketball player.

Chapter 6: Legacy and Future

Ja Morant, as young as he is, still has a legacy of his own to carve in the NBA. He is yet to truly establish his own legacy, as he is still creating his own unique identity in the league, although he has already begun to show what type of player he is. That said, while he may still be creating his own legacy, he is also a legacy player in the sense that he is someone who learned from the other players that came before him.

It is difficult to not compare Morant to some of the most athletic point guards in the history of the game. Before Stephen Curry changed the game into a jump-shooting league and before point guards started focusing on their jump shots, the NBA saw in the influx of athletic point guards that had a good combination of size, speed, and explosiveness. This happened sometime during the late 2000s and the early 2010s.

Players like Derrick Rose, Russell Westbrook, and John Wall changed the point guard position in their own way because of how they toyed with their defenders by using their size and athleticism to their advantage. To this day, there are videos on YouTube that showcase all of their unbelievable athletic plays during their respective primes.

However, videos of the likes of Rose, Westbrook, and Wall in younger players are not as prevalent nowadays because it takes good genetics and the proper training to be as athletic as they are. On top of that, most of the younger point guards would rather emulate Stephen Curry. But Ja Morant is someone who broke the mold because he did not want to be Stephen Curry. Even before he grew into his athleticism, he idolized the likes of Russell Westbrook above any other point guard in the league. And when he grew to become 6'3" with a vertical leaping ability that was, for lack of a better description, out of this world, that was when he truly became similar to Westbrook and all of the other athletic point guards that came before him.

It is true that Morant's game is similar to that of the other athletic point guards that blaze the trail for him. He continues their legacy because he proves that explosive point guards still have a place in a league dominated by playmakers that focus more on being like Stephen Curry with his shooting or Kyrie Irving with his handles. There are good reasons why he is the flag bearer of the athletic point guard playing style. He is just as quick and fast as John Wall. He knows how to be shifty and elusive like Derrick Rose. He can jump out of the roof like Russell Westbrook. All those can be seen in how he attacks the basket relentlessly and in the way he goes after centers and power forwards alike with vicious dunk attempts or acrobatic layups near the basket.

Despite being a great finisher and scorer, Morant could also dish the ball at the level of a John Wall. He can even grab rebounds well enough at his size and position, even though he is not the same kind of rebounder as Westbrook. And that makes him a great all-around player.

He may be known for his athletic abilities and ridiculous finishes at the basket, but Morant has a finesse side to his game as well, especially when it comes to the floaters he tends to throw up in the lane whenever defenders are too close to the basket. His floaters are reminiscent of what Derrick Rose used to do during his prime years. As such, while plenty of people compare Ja Morant's athleticism and explosiveness to Russell Westbrook's, he has the skills and shiftiness of a prime Derrick Rose. Morant could have been what Rose should have been had he stayed healthy. And the fact that he has the nuclear athleticism of Westbrook and the finesse of Rose makes him an entirely unique player.

But what truly makes Durant a unique player is the fact that he has the makings of someone who could be a respectable or even a good three-point shooter. He may never be a Stephen Curry or even a Damian Lillard when it comes to his jump shot, but Morant has the tools and the jumper that would allow him to become a shooter that defenders would never gamble on. Once Morant adds that tool to his growing arsenal, it should be game over for the league.

In terms of his fearless mindset and confidence, one can also compare Morant to Allen Iverson. Barely six feet tall and with his slight frame, Iverson was never afraid to go up against the biggest and strongest players in the history of the league. He was not the most efficient scorer, but he could put points in a hurry because he was not afraid to take his shots, even when he needed to do so against bigger defenders in the paint.

Allen Iverson's confidence, fearlessness, and slight frame are evident in Morant, who always plays with a chip on his shoulder and is never afraid of the biggest moment. The way he attacks the basket and goes after any kind of defense he sees is reminiscent of what Iverson used to do during his prime. And that is why some fans also love to say that Morant is a bigger and more athletic version of Iverson minus the inefficient shot attempts. Nevertheless, Morant is becoming a unique player in his own right, with his combination of athleticism, finesse, fearlessness, and potential all in a slight frame.

Most of the other athletic All-Star point guards that came before him were muscular beasts that relied almost entirely on their athletic gifts. But Morant is someone who has the makings of a player that could be better than them despite being skinnier. That is due to his hardworking mentality and relentless quest to become better. As long as he is willing to accept that he still has weaknesses in his game, he will never stop trying to improve, and that will make him a point guard that could very well be unique in the sense that he could finish at the basket, make graceful plays, hit jump shots, and create plays for others.

Morant also has the makings of someone who could become the greatest player in the Memphis Grizzlies' history. There have not been many All-Stars that have played for Memphis. Even if the Grizzlies had a star, they did not stay too long or were not great scorers. Arguably their greatest players are Mike Conley and Marc Gasol, who both are not known for putting up significant numbers. And Conley is the franchise's all-time leading scorer. Given that Morant is already second all-time in franchise triple-doubles and is just in the early stages of his career, he could very well be at the top of the leaderboard in almost every statistic in Grizzlies' franchise history except for blocks and rebounds. He is on pace to become an even better scorer than Mike Conley, and that could happen anytime soon as long as he stays healthy and is willing to commit to the franchise on a long-term basis.

The outlook for Ja Morant and the Memphis Grizzlies seems bright because this franchise has never had a player with the talent and potential that he possesses. And as long as he stays healthy and continues to work on his game while carrying the Grizzlies in his ascent to the top, the franchise's first-ever MVP award might be in the books for Ja Morant. And if he is playing at the level of an MVP, the franchise's first-ever championship should also be a possibility as well. The future for Morant and the Grizzlies can be as high as where his legs can take him in the air.

Final Word/About the Author

I was born and raised in Norwalk, Connecticut. Growing up, I could often be found spending many nights watching basketball, soccer, and football matches with my father in the family living room. I love sports and everything that sports can embody. I believe that sports are one of the most genuine forms of competition, heart, and determination. I write my works to learn more about influential athletes in the hopes that from my writing, you the reader can walk away inspired to put in an equal if not greater amount of hard work and perseverance to pursue your goals. If you enjoyed *Ja Morant: The Inspiring Story of One of Basketball's All-Star Point Guards,* please leave a review! Also, you can read more of my works on *David Ortiz, Mike Trout, Bryce Harper, Jackie Robinson, Aaron Judge, Odell Beckham Jr., Bill Belichick, Serena Williams, Rafael Nadal, Roger Federer, Novak Djokovic, Richard Sherman, Andrew Luck, Rob Gronkowski, Brett Favre, Calvin Johnson,*

Drew Brees, J.J. Watt, Colin Kaepernick, Aaron Rodgers, Peyton Manning, Tom Brady, Russell Wilson, Odell Beckham Jr., Bill Belichick, Charles Barkley, Trae Young, Gregg Popovich, Pat Riley, John Wooden, Steve Kerr, Brad Stevens, Red Auerbach, Doc Rivers, Erik Spoelstra, Michael Jordan, LeBron James, Kyrie Irving, Klay Thompson, Stephen Curry, Kevin Durant, Russell Westbrook, Anthony Davis, Chris Paul, Blake Griffin, Kobe Bryant, Joakim Noah, Scottie Pippen, Carmelo Anthony, Kevin Love, Grant Hill, Tracy McGrady, Vince Carter, Patrick Ewing, Karl Malone, Tony Parker, Allen Iverson, Hakeem Olajuwon, Reggie Miller, Michael Carter-Williams, John Wall, James Harden, Tim Duncan, Steve Nash, Draymond Green, Kawhi Leonard, Dwyane Wade, Ray Allen, Pau Gasol, Dirk Nowitzki, Jimmy Butler, Paul Pierce, Manu Ginobili, Pete Maravich, Larry Bird, Kyle Lowry, Jason Kidd, David Robinson, LaMarcus Aldridge, Derrick Rose, Paul George, Kevin Garnett, Chris Paul, Marc Gasol, Yao Ming, Al Horford,

Amar'e Stoudemire, DeMar DeRozan, Isaiah Thomas, Kemba Walker, Chris Bosh, Andre Drummond, JJ Redick, DeMarcus Cousins, Wilt Chamberlain, Bradley Beal, Rudy Gobert, Aaron Gordon, Kristaps Porzingis, Nikola Vucevic, Andre Iguodala, Devin Booker, John Stockton, Jeremy Lin, Chris Paul, Pascal Siakam, Jayson Tatum, Gordon Hayward, Nikola Jokic, Bill Russell, Victor Oladipo, Luka Doncic, Ben Simmons, Shaquille O'Neal, Joel Embiid, Donovan Mitchell, Damian Lillard and *Giannis Antetokounmpo* in the Kindle Store. If you love basketball, check out my website at claytongeoffreys.com to join my exclusive list where I let you know about my latest books and give you lots of goodies.

Like what you read? Please leave a review!

I write because I love sharing the stories of influential athletes like Ja Morant with fantastic readers like you. My readers inspire me to write more so please do not hesitate to let me know what you thought by leaving a review! If you love books on life, basketball, or productivity, check out my website at claytongeoffreys.com to join my exclusive list where I let you know about my latest books. Aside from being the first to hear about my latest releases, you can also download a free copy of *33 Life Lessons: Success Principles, Career Advice & Habits of Successful People.* See you there!

Clayton

References

[i] Yates, Clinton. "Ja Morant: Point God from the back road". *The Undefeated.* 20 June 2019. Web.

[ii] Sandlin, Blake. "Making Morant: Ja Morant's ascent from small town kid to big stage star". *Murray State News.* 1 March 2019. Web.

[iii] Norlander, Matt. "Court Report: The real story of Ja Morant and Zion Williamson playing on the same AAU team". *CBS.* 23 January 2019. Web.

[iv] Forde, Pat. "How a hungry coach led to the discovery of viral college sensation Ja Morant". *Yahoo Sports.* 30 January 2019. Web.

[v] Forde, Pat. "From mid-major to top-two NBA draft pick: Ja Morant's historic rise". *Yahoo Sports.* 19 June 2019. Web.

[vi] West, Jenna. "Ja Morant ends season as first player in NCAA history to average 20 points, 10 assists". *Sports Illustrated.* 23 March 2019. Web.

[vii] Wasserman, Jonathan. "Ja Morant's 2019 NBA Draft Scouting report: analysis of Grizzlies pick". *Bleacher Report.* 21 June 2019. Web.

[viii] "Visual timeline of the day that changed everything: March 11". *ESPN.* 11 March 2021. Web.

[ix] Carlson, Cassie. "Ja Morant packs on 12 pounds over NBA's hiatus". *Action News 5.* 3 July 2020. Web.

[x] Dupont, Zach. "Ja Morant on potentially being an All-Star: 'I Deserve This. I Earned This'". *Slam Online.* 26 January 2022. Web.

Made in the USA
Monee, IL
27 June 2022